Jesus AND Moses

THE PARALLEL SAYINGS

"Joey Green shows us the commonalities between Judaism and Christianity—a crucial undertaking in today's troubled world—by focusing on some of the richest and most resonant words of wisdom from the writings of both faiths. The result is a book full of insight, compassion, and loving-kindness, and a healthy reminder that there are far more similarities than differences in the core values of Christians and Jews."

—JONATHAN KIRSCH, AUTHOR OF *THE WOMAN WHO LAUGHED AT GOD* AND *MOSES: A LIFE*

"As someone who teaches Judaism to both Jews and Christians, this book will be an invaluable source for students in understanding the common teachings of both Judaism and Christianity. I recommend this book to serious students of religion as well as to the public at large."

—RABBI NEAL WEINBERG, DIRECTOR OF THE MILLER INTRODUCTION TO JUDAISM PROGRAM, UNIVERSITY OF JUDAISM, LOS ANGELES

"This helpful juxtaposition of Christian and Jewish biblical sources is made accessible to those who seek scriptural evidence of the similarity and difference of Judaism and Christianity. In an era of spiritual globalization, this is a valuable contribution."

—RABBI HAROLD M. SCHULWEIS, AUTHOR OF *FOR THOSE WHO CANNOT BELIEVE*

Jesus AND Moses

THE PARALLEL SAYINGS

EDITOR
Joey Green

FOREWORD
Rabbi Stewart Vogel

Seastone

First Ulysses Press Edition 2002

Published by:
Seastone, an imprint of Ulysses Press
P.O. Box 3440
Berkeley, CA 94703
www.ulyssespress.com

The publishers have generously given permission to use quotations from the works cited on page 189.

Library of Congress Cataloging-in-Publication Data

Jesus and Moses : the parallel sayings / editor, Joey Green ; introduction, Stewart Vogel.-- 1st Ulysses Press ed.

p. cm.
Includes bibliographical references.
ISBN 1-56975-303-2

1. Bible. N.T. Gospels--Relation to the Old Testament. 2. Bible. O.T.--Relation to the Gospels. 3. Bible. N.T. Gospels--Extra-canonical parallels. 4. Rabbinical literature--Relation to the New Testament. 5. Christianity and other religions--Judaism. 6. Judaism--Relations--Christianity. I. Green, Joey.

BS2387 .J47 2001
226'.06--dc21   2001057623

Printed in Canada by Transcontinental Printing

10 9 8 7 6 5 4 3 2 1

Project Editor: Ray Riegert
Senior Editor: Richard Harris
Design: Leslie Henriques and Big Fish

Distributed in the United States by Publishers Group West and in Canada by Raincoast Books.

For Deborah

A C K N O W L E D G E M E N T S

At Ulysses Press, I am deeply indebted to project editor Ray Riegert and senior editor Richard Harris for their guidance. For their sage advice, ideas, insights, and teachings, I am grateful to Rabbi Neal Weinberg and Librarian Haim Gottshalk at the University of Judaism in Bel Air, California; Rabbi Stewart Vogel and Rabbi Tsafreer Lev at Temple Aliyah in Woodland Hills, California; Rabbi Jay Levy at Kol Tikvah in Woodland Hills, California; and Rabbi Ed Feinstein and Librarian Helene Gersuk at Valley Beth Shalom in Encino, California; Reverend Robert Schwarz at Saint Ann's Church in Sayville, New York; Claire Chun at Ulysses Press; my agent Jeremy Solomon; and my brilliant mother, Barbara Green. Above all, all my love to Debbie, Ashley, and Julia.

—Joey Green

CONTENTS

FOREWORD
By Rabbi Stewart Vogel

This book provides an excellent opportunity for anyone to compare some of the most important ideas of Judaism and Christianity. The astute juxtaposition of texts beautifully illustrates the areas of commonality and distinction between the world's earliest monotheistic traditions.

While the title *Jesus and Moses* suggests a comparison of direct quotes from the two great religious leaders, this book utilizes material in the Jewish sections from Biblical and rabbinic writings that post-date Moses. Does this method provide a legitimate comparison? Whether you believe in the long-held Jewish view that both the Written Law (Torah) and Oral Law (rabbinic writings of the Talmud) were given to Moses by God at Mount Sinai or whether you recognize that post-Mosaic Judaism sees itself inspired by the Sinaitic revelation, these passages provide opportunities for comparison otherwise not available. In these cases, Moses becomes the persona of a Jewish view that allows for a comparison to Jesus who comes nearly thirteen hundred years later.

Many Biblical studies rely on personal interpretation, and Joey Green has tapped into his own relationship to the Jewish and Christian texts to establish connections of content and style. This approach is intentionally less academic, but unquestionably more meaningful to the average reader. The final product is a book containing ideas that have not only influenced the lives of millions of individuals, but also helped to shape Christianity and Judaism. With this book, you can explore the richness of these religious traditions and find inspiration for your daily life.

How many books offer words that have brought meaning to millions over the millennia? By culling through the Christian and Jewish sources, Joey Green has brought easy access to the best of both traditions.

It is a shame that two traditions that enjoy such a common language and promote love of the "stranger" and "neighbor" should have such a history of conflict. I hope this book will help you gain a new appreciation for your own religious tradition as well as that of your "neighbor." Whether you are Christian, Jewish, Muslim, Buddhist, Hindu, Sikh, or any other religion, this book has the potential to inspire and bring a new understanding that we are all made in the image of God.

INTRODUCTION

Jesus of Nazareth needs no introduction. He is unquestionably the most famous Jew in the world.

Jesus was a Jew who taught Judaism to Jews in the Galilean towns and villages in Roman-occupied Judea during the time of the Second Temple.

In the New Testament, Jesus is born to a Jewish mother, is circumcised eight days after his birth in accord with Jewish law, wears tzitzit (ritual fringes) on his clothes, puts on tefillin (phylacteries) at morning prayers, looks upon God as his heavenly Father, keeps kosher, observes the Jewish Sabbath and all the ceremonial laws, teaches Jewish ethics in synagogues, is called Rabbi ("teacher"), and makes a pilgrimage to Jerusalem for Passover. At the Last Supper (a Passover seder), he blesses the wine and bread, dips the herbs into the charosets, drinks four cups of wine, and recites Hallel (a group of Psalms). Even having hand-picked disciples was common among rabbis at the time.

Biblical scholars debate whether Jesus was a member of the Essenes (a small Jewish monastic sect living on the shores of the Dead Sea) or the Pharisees (the Rabbinic Sages who studied and interpreted the Torah). But all agree Jesus was a rabbi who was well-versed in Judaism and preached traditional Jewish ethics to Jews.

Jesus was undoubtedly an excellent teacher with an exceptional gift for coining pithy sayings and crafting lively parables—a common teaching device in his day. He taught illiterate Jewish peasants the pure essence of Judaism. He gleaned the most pivotal ethical teachings from the Hebrew Bible, the Apocrypha (the books rejected from the Hebrew Bible), and the Psuedepigrapha (Jewish writings produced during the era of Jewish Hellenism). Jesus condensed these ethical teachings, simplified them, and eloquently popularized them, making them accessible to a larger audience. He also embraced the ideas of the great Rabbinic Sages of his time, whose parallel teachings can be found in the Talmud (a detailed commentary on the Hebrew Bible composed over seven centuries) and Midrashic literature (Rabbinic stories to explain missing information from the Hebrew Bible). In almost every case, the ethical teachings of Jesus match the ethical teachings of Judaism—from before, during, and after his lifetime.

Judaism does, however, vehemently disagree with a handful of Jesus's teachings. Unlike Jesus, Judaism allows retaliation against evil and insists that only God forgives sins committed against Him. While Jesus expected the imminent establishment of God's kingdom on earth and the accompanying resurrection of the dead (both common Jewish beliefs among Pharisees and Essenes at the time), Jesus and his disciples also believed him to be the Messiah.

The Romans considered any potential Messiah to be a political rebel, and Pontius Pilate, the cruel and brutal Roman governor of Judea, ordered that Jesus be crucified, the standard Roman method of executing political revolutionaries. Pilate then ordered the sign "King of the Jews" be nailed to the cross over Jesus as a warning to any other would-be Messiahs that an agonizing death awaited them. Other would-be Messiahs who rose up against and were subsequently killed by the Romans—before and after Jesus—included Judas the Galilean

(6 C.E.), Theduas (44 C.E.), Benjamin the Egyptian (circa 60 C.E.), Menachem (67 C.E.) and Bar Kochba (135 C.E.). Some Biblical scholars agree that the gospel writers intentionally distorted the story of the trial and crucifixion of Jesus in the New Testament, placing blame on the Jews rather than the Romans, in order to convert the pagan Romans to Christianity and to avoid Roman persecution. Unfortunately, this distortion caused centuries of persecution and genocide against the Jews, including the Crusades, the Spanish Inquisition, Russian pogroms, and the Holocaust.

The Jewish conception of the Messiah also differs greatly from the Christian conception of the Messiah. To Jews, the Messiah is a human military leader who will bring all the Jews back to live in Israel and put an end to hate, war, poverty, and disease. The majority of Jews today dismiss the idea of a Messiah and instead believe that people must all work together to bring about a Messianic Age—an enlightened level of spiritual evolution. Christianity radically altered the Jewish concept of the Messiah. In the New Testament, the Messiah became the Son of God who died for the sins of mankind. To Jews, worshipping any man as God or the Son of God is a blasphemous concept. To Jews, Jesus was an exceptionally gifted and wise rabbi—not a prophet, not the Messiah, not the Son of God, not God Himself. This is a huge gap.

While the differences between Judaism and Christianity are immense, the similarities are equally enormous. At their core, the ethical teachings of both religions stem from a deeply shared morality. Christians are indebted to Judaism for shaping Jesus's teachings. Jews are indebted to Christianity for making the Hebrew Bible a universal book that has influenced Western civilization and spread the light of Jewish ethics around the world. Jews are also grateful to the Catholic Church for preserving a vast library of Jewish literary treasures, including the Apocrypha, the Pseudepigrapha, and the writings of Josephus and Philo. While Judaism does not accept Jesus as the Messiah, Jews can embrace Jesus as a gifted teacher of Jewish ethics, a great artist in parable, and an advocate of uncompromising morality, integrity, and compassion. Likewise, Christians can spiritually and intellectually benefit from a deeper understanding of Judaism.

Here then for the first time—laid side by side for easy comparison—are the ethical teachings of Jesus and the parallel ethical teachings of Judaism that emanate from the divine call to Moses at Mount Sinai. Jews will be awed to discover the intense Jewishness of Jesus's sayings. Christians will be astonished to discover how remarkably Jesus's teachings echo the wisdom of Jewish Sages. I hope this brings us all closer together with a renewed respect for our differences and a deeper appreciation for the beauty of our shared heritage.

The quotes in this book attributed to Jesus are culled from the four gospels of the New Testament, written in Aramaic and Greek many years after the crucifixion of Jesus. Tradition holds that the gospels were written by Matthew (one of the apostles), Mark (a disciple from Jerusalem), Luke (a former pagan who accompanied Paul on his missionary travels), and John (another apostle). Church scholars declared the present books of the New Testament as authoritative

Scripture by 400 C.E. No writings by Jesus himself are known to exist. Biblical scholars claim that the story of Jesus was transmitted orally for many years and the gospels were then written, rewritten, and revised by a number of writers. Many scholars question whether any New Testament writers knew Jesus personally. While the gospels frequently contradict each other and are sometimes inconsistent with historical fact, the New Testament remains the only source of the teachings of Jesus universally accepted by all Christian denominations. Several Christian apocryphal books—most notably the Gospel of Thomas and the Gospel of Philip (both discovered in 1945 by two peasant brothers near Nag Hammadi, Egypt)—contain sayings attributed to Jesus. However, I have selected the quotes from Jesus for this book only from sources recognized as authentic by all mainstream Christian denominations.

Many of the quotes in this book attributed to Moses can be found in the Torah (the Five Books of Moses in the Hebrew Bible). According to Jewish tradition, Moses was the sole author of the Torah, which was revealed to him by God on Mount Sinai. Biblical scholars, however, insist that the Torah was also written, rewritten, and revised by a number of authors and ultimately edited by Ezra the Scribe in 444 B.C.E.

Other quotes attributed to Moses in this book are actually Rabbinic writings that post-date Moses by centuries. According to the traditional Jewish view, God revealed both the Written Law (Torah) and Oral Law to Moses at Mount Sinai. Centuries later, Rabbinic Sages put the Oral Law into writing, creating the Mishna. The Mishna, composed of sixty-three sections (called tractates) was written between 70 C.E. and 200 C.E., and was compiled and systematically codified by

Rabbi Judah the Prince around 220 C.E. The Talmud, one of the great literary works of all time, is a detailed commentary on the Mishna composed over several centuries by scholars working in academies in Babylon and Jerusalem. Rabbinic Sages completed the Jerusalem Talmud around 425 C.E. and the Babylonian Talmud around 500 C.E. The Talmud is also considered an expansion of Mosaic wisdom.

The Oral Law was also committed to writing in the Midrash. A Midrash is a story to explain missing information from the Hebrew Bible and interpret the Scripture to extract deeper meanings. Collections of Midrashic literature include Sifre Zuta (third century C.E.), Sifre, Sifra, Mekhilta, Mekhilta de Rabbi Simeon bar Yohai (fourth century C.E.), Tanhuma (fifth century C.E.), Pesikta Rabbati (845 C.E.), Pesikta of Rabbi Kahana (circa ninth century C.E.), Pesikta Zutarta (eleventh century C.E.), Midrash Rabbah (from third to twelfth century C.E.), and Midrash ha-Gadol and Yalkut Shimoni (thirteenth century C.E.).

Other Jewish wisdom literature omitted from the Hebrew Bible sprang from this same Mosaic tradition. The Wisdom of Ben Sirah (Ecclesiasticus in Greek), a book of proverbs penned by the Jewish Sage and teacher Jesus ben Sirah (circa 185 B.C.E.), influenced the writers of the Talmud and was incorporated into the Greek version of Bible. The Testaments of the Twelve Patriarchs, a Jewish psuedepigraphical work purporting to be the testaments of the twelve sons of Jacob, was written in Hebrew and Aramaic during the second century B.C.E.

Other works considered to hold Mosaic authority include the writings of Philo (circa 25 B.C.E.–40 C.E.), a Jewish-Alexandrian philosopher who wrote about the greatness of Jewish scripture and Mosaic law and infused Hellenistic ideas and values into Jewish tradition; Seder Eliyahu, a collection of moral homilies (probably written in the tenth century C.E.); and the Zohar, a kabbalistic work focusing on mystical interpretations of biblical passages, primarily written by Moses de Leon toward the end of the thirteenth century C.E. (although authorship is often attributed to Simeon bar Yohai and his contemporaries).

Collectively, all these inspired writings become the voice of Moses.

Parallel Sayings,
Parallel Worlds

"Hear O Israel, the Lord our God, the Lord is One."

"Love the Lord your God with all your heart, with all your soul, and with all your might."

"Love your neighbor as yourself."

These revolutionary teachings, first articulated by Moses in the Hebrew Bible, were reiterated thirteen hundred years later by Jesus in the New Testament.

While the epic stories of both Jesus and Moses depict supernatural events, both men are portrayed as phenomenal teachers with divinely-inspired religious sensibilities. Moses develops the concept of ethical monotheism, insisting that the One God demands that man, created in His spiritual image, must emulate God's virtues—namely love, justice, and mercy. Moses ingeniously creates a system of rituals to turn a group of liberated Hebrew slaves into a holy people with high ethical and moral standards—giving them the Torah. Jesus passionately preaches love, mercy, justice, and forgiveness, and is portrayed in the gospels as initiating an emphasis on the ethical aspects of Judaism over the ritual practices. Although many of Jesus's teachings can be found in the Hebrew Bible and the Talmud, his love for the spirit of Jewish law—rather than the letter of the law—has profoundly influenced humanity.

The life stories of Moses and Jesus get off to a similar start. In the Book of Exodus, the Pharaoh orders the Egyptians to kill all male Israelite babies. The infant Moses escapes the genocidal decree because his mother puts him in a basket and sets it on the Nile River. In the Gospel of Matthew, King Herod orders all male children in the Bethlehem area killed. The infant Jesus escapes the murderous decree because his parents flee with him to Egypt. Just as nothing is known about Moses's youth other than that he was raised in Egypt as son of the Pharaoh's daughter, nothing is known of Jesus's youth except that he was raised in Nazareth by Joseph and Mary who brought him at the age of twelve to Jerusalem for Passover, where he got lost and was found debating in the Temple.

Some biblical scholars theorize that the writers of the gospels intentionally infused the story of Jesus with parallels to the life of Moses to better show Jesus as the fulfillment of the prophecies of the Hebrew Bible—a new Moses.

Moses parts the Sea of Reeds; Jesus walks on the Sea of Galilee. Moses receives the Ten Commandments on Mount Sinai; Jesus delivers the Sermon on the Mount. Moses spends forty days and forty nights on Mount Sinai; Jesus fasts for forty days and forty nights in the wilderness. Moses receives manna and quails to feed six-hundred thousand men and makes water flow from a rock; Jesus divides two fish and seven loaves of bread among more than five thousand people. Moses leads the twelve tribes of Israel to the Promised Land; Jesus chooses twelve disciples. Moses declares the last supper in Egypt to be the Passover feast, a meal to be used as a remembrance of the bondage in

Egypt and how God freed the Israelite slaves; at the Last Supper in Jerusalem, Jesus gives two symbols of the Passover seder new meaning: he proclaims that the bread is his body and the wine is his blood.

Even if the gospel writers did not purposefully imbue the story of Jesus with elements that parallel the story of Moses, similarities between the lives of the two great leaders abound. In the Hebrew Bible, Moses helps free the Hebrew slaves from bondage in Egypt, establishes a new system of ethical and moral laws, and leads the Israelites to the Promised Land. In the New Testament, Jesus tries to help the Jews transcend Roman oppression on a spiritual level by teaching high standards of ethical behavior to create a kingdom of heaven on earth.

On a literary level, each story scathingly attacks an oppressive empire. In the story of Moses, the ten plagues can be interpreted as a satiric assault on the gods of Egypt. Passages in The Wisdom of Solomon, a Hellenistic-Jewish work from the Apocrypha, identify the ten plagues as punishment to mock Egyptian paganism. The ancient Egyptians deified the Nile River, the life source of the people, as Hapi the Nile god. They saw the annual rising of the Nile as the work of the great god Osiris. From a literary perspective, turning the Nile to blood negated these two Egyptian gods. The killing of all the frogs of the second plague can be seen as a mockery of the well-known Egyptian frog goddess Heqt, who assisted women in labor. Combined, the first two plagues become poetic retribution for the decree of the pharaoh ordering every Hebrew infant boy to be drowned in the Nile River. Taken together, all the plagues mock the power of the pharaoh—a self-proclaimed god, whose divinity was sustained by the religious and political institutions of Egypt. The ninth plague, darkness for three days, mocks the Egyptian sun god Re, regarded as the most important god and the father of the first pharaoh, from whom all other pharaohs were descended.

Similarly, the story of Jesus can be seen as a poignant indictment of the barbarism and ruthlessness of the Romans who ruled over Judea. During the first century C.E., the Romans condemned 50,000 to 100,000 Jews to death by crucifixion—a brutal form of execution forbidden by Jewish law because it was torture. Against the backdrop of Rome's tyrannical rule, Jesus shines as a beacon of compassion, love, and forgiveness. This contrast becomes horrifically apparent when the Romans whip and torture the gentle Jesus, thrust a crown of thorns on his head, nail him to a crucifix, and then heartlessly cast dice for his clothes. On a literary level, the crucifixion of Jesus mocks the Romans as sadistic barbarians who would torture and kill the Son of God. Jesus responds to this atrocity with the ultimate plea for compassion; he looks heavenward and cries, "Father, forgive them, for they do not know what they are doing" (Luke 23:34).

Both stories also focus on the notion of divine justice. The story of Moses begins with the Egyptians committing genocide on the Israelites by drowning every Hebrew male infant in the Nile River. In retribution, the first plague God inflicts upon the Egyptians is turning the Nile River to blood—bringing the atrocity to the surface. The final plague God unleashes upon the Egyptians is the death of every first-born Egyptian male child. As Jesus insists in the New Testament, "With the measure you use, it will be measured to you" (Matthew 7:2).

For all the similarities between Moses and Jesus, the differences in the lives of the two men are equally significant. Moses establishes the freed Israelite slaves as a nation under his leadership for forty years in the wilderness; Jesus never leads the Jewish people or frees them from Roman oppression. Moses kills an Egyptian taskmaster and escapes arrest; Jesus is arrested and sentenced to death unjustly by the Romans for being a potential revolutionary. Moses tells the Pharaoh "Let my people go" and unleashes ten plagues upon the Egyptians; Jesus never makes any demands of Pontius Pilate and does not unleash any plagues on the Romans. Moses marries Zipporah and has two sons, Gershom and Eliazar; Jesus remains single and childless. Moses has sinners stoned to death; Jesus prevents people from stoning others. Moses oversees battles; Jesus remains a pacifist. Moses sees the Israelites lapse into idolatry, worshipping a golden calf; Jesus experiences no such pagan activity among the Jews—although he does express similar outrage against the moneychangers and those selling pigeons in the Temple.

The most striking difference between Jesus and Moses is how the two religious heroes take their respective places in Christianity and Judaism. Jesus is crucified by the Romans while in his thirties, rises from the dead, and ascends to heaven, where He sits at the right hand of the Father. Moses, however, remains a fallible human being. He dies of natural causes alone in the land of Moab at 120 years of age and, as the Book of Deuteronomy tells us, "no one knows his burial place to this day"—preventing the Jews from worshipping Moses or turning him into a deity.

Despite the differences in their life stories, Jesus and Moses both preached against injustice, advocated compassion for the poor, and urged their followers to love one another. They were both inspiring teachers determined to raise mankind to a higher spiritual level and instill us all with love and awe for God. The light of their teachings remains eternal. Jesus could have easily been speaking for Moses when he said, "Heaven and earth will pass away, but my words will never pass away."

The Parallel Sayings

Love

It is frequently said—and wrongly so—that Judaism is a religion of strict laws and harsh discipline while Christianity is a religion of love and compassion.

In truth, love is an essential ingredient of both religions. Moses tells us to "love the Lord your God with all your heart, and with all your soul, and with all your might" (Deuteronomy 6:5). The golden rule, to love your neighbor as yourself, also originates as a commandment told by God to Moses (Leviticus 19:18). Jesus embraces these teachings as the two most important commandments. To the rabbis of the Talmud, love for your neighbor translates to love for all humanity—a natural extension of your love of God.

Not surprisingly, Jesus—a contemporary of the great Rabbis of the Talmud—advocated love of God and all humanity, a tradition already sanctified in Judaism. God's love for humanity is expressed throughout the Hebrew Bible just as it is in the New Testament—as the love of a father for his children. "All men are created in the divine image," stated the second-century C.E. teacher Simeon ben Azzai, "and, therefore, all are our fellow men, and entitled to human love."

Blessed are those who mourn, for they will be comforted.

MATTHEW 5:3

Those who sow in tears will reap in songs of joy.

PSALM 126:5

Blessed are the merciful, for they will be shown mercy.

MATTHEW 5:3

He who has mercy on others will be shown mercy by heaven.

BABYLONIAN TALMUD: SHABBAT 151B

Blessed are the peacemakers, for they will be called sons of God.

MATTHEW 5:9

Be of the disciples of Aaron—loving peace and pursuing peace, loving your fellow-creatures, and drawing them near to Torah.

HILLEL: MISHNA: PIRKE AVOT I:12

If anyone strikes you on the right cheek, turn to him the other also.

LUKE 6:28

Better to be one of the persecuted than one of the persecutors.

BABYLONIAN TALMUD: BABA KAMA 93A

You have heard that it was said, "Love your neighbor and hate your enemy."* But I tell you: Love your enemies, and pray for those who persecute you, that you may be sons of your Father in heaven.

MATTHEW 5:43-45

You shall not take vengeance or bear a grudge against your kinfolk. Love your neighbor as yourself.

LEVITICUS 19:18

* *The commandment "hate your enemy" does not appear in the Hebrew Bible or any rabbinic literature.*

He causes his sun to rise on the evil and the good, and sends rain on the righteous and the unrighteous.

MATTHEW 5:45

The rain falls both for the righteous and for the wicked.

BABYLONIAN TALMUD: TAANIT 7A

If you love those who love you, what reward will you get? Are not even the tax collectors doing that? Do not even pagans do that?

MATTHEW 5:46-47

When a stranger resides with you in your land, you shall not wrong him. The stranger who resides with you shall be to you as one of your citizens; you shall love him as yourself, for you were strangers in the land of Egypt.

LEVITICUS 19:33-34

Consider the ravens: They do not sow or reap, they have no storeroom or barn, yet God feeds them.

LUKE 12:24

He who created the day also created the sustenance for it.

MIDRASH: MEKHILTA: BESHALLAH: VA-YISU 2

Ask, and it will be given you; seek, and you will find; knock, and the door will be opened to you. For everyone who asks receives; he who seeks finds; and to him who knocks, the door will be opened.

LUKE 11:9-10

I love those who love Me,
And those who seek Me find Me.

PROVERBS 8:17

Freely you have received, freely give.

MATTHEW 10:8

Just as God is merciful and gracious, so you be merciful and gracious, bestowing these gifts freely to everyone. Just as the Lord is called righteous and loving, so you be righteous and loving.

MIDRASH: SIFRE DEUTERONOMY 85A

If your brother sins against you, go and show him his fault, just between the two of you. If he listens to you, you have won your brother over.

MATTHEW 18:15

Love one another from the heart, therefore, and if anyone sins against you, speak to him in peace. Expel the venom of hatred, and do not harbor deceit in your heart. If anyone confesses and repents, forgive him.

TESTAMENTS OF THE TWELVE PATRIARCHS: GAD 6:3

The most important [commandment] is this: "Hear O Israel, the Lord our God, the Lord is One. Love the Lord your God with all your heart, and with all your soul, and with all your might." The second is this: "Love your neighbor as yourself." There is no commandment greater than these.

MARK 12:29-31

Hear, O Israel! The Lord our God, the Lord is one. You shall love the Lord your God with all your heart, and with all your soul, and with all your might.

DEUTERONOMY 6:4-5

"Love your neighbor as yourself" (Leviticus 19:18). Rabbi Akiva says, "This is the great principal of the Torah."

JERUSALEM TALMUD: NEDARIM 9:4:ID-E

O Jerusalem, Jerusalem, you who kill the prophets and stone those sent to you, how often I have longed to gather your children together, as a hen gathers her chicks under her wings, but you were not willing.

Luke 13:34

And the Lord said to Moses, "How long will this people spurn Me, and how long will they have no faith in Me despite all the signs that I have performed in their midst?"

Numbers 14:11

Who are my mother and brothers? . . . Here are my mother and brothers. Whoever does God's will is my brother and sister and mother.

MARK 3:33-35

Who said of his father, and of his mother,
"I consider them not."
His brothers he disregarded,
Ignored his own children.
Your precepts alone they observed,
And kept Your covenant.

DEUTERONOMY 33:9

Do you see this woman? I came into your house. You did not give me any water for my feet, but she wet my feet with her tears and wiped them with her hair. You did not give me a kiss, but this woman, from the time I entered, has not stopped kissing my feet. You did not put oil on my head, but she has poured perfume on my feet. Therefore, I tell you, her many sins have been forgiven—for she loved much. But he who has been forgiven little loves little.

LUKE 7:44-47

If a man gives the finest gifts in the world to a needy person but does so with a sullen countenance, it is as if he gave nothing; but he who receives a needy person with a cheerful countenance, even if he is unable to give him anything, has given him the finest gifts in the world.

BABYLONIAN TALMUD: AVOT DE RABBI NATHAN 13:4

Peace be to this house.

LUKE 10:5

The Lord bless you and keep you!

The Lord make His face to shine upon you and be gracious to you!

The Lord lift up His countenance to you and grant you peace!

NUMBERS 6:24-26

Father, forgive them, for they do not know what they are
doing.

LUKE 23:34

⎯⎯ ⎯⎯

If anyone wishes to do you harm, you should pray for him,
along with doing good, and you will be rescued by the Lord
from every evil.

TESTAMENTS OF THE TWELVE PATRIARCHS: JOSEPH 18:2

A new command I give you: Love one another.

JOHN 13:34

A new command I give you: Love one another.

Love your neighbor as yourself.

LEVITICUS 19:18

Greater love has no one than this, that he lay down his life for his friends.

JOHN 15:13

A war ended, leaving two friends in two separate kingdoms. When one friend tried to secretly visit the other, he was captured, accused of being a spy, and sentenced to death by the king. The man begged the king to let him go for one month so he could make arrangements for his family. He promised to return to face the death penalty. "What assurance do I have that you will return?" asked the king.

The man answered, "Send for my friend. He will stay in prison for me while I am gone, and if I do not return, he will pay for my life with his own life." To the king's astonishment, the friend agreed to the arrangement.

A month later, the king's executioner was about to kill the imprisoned friend with his sword. Suddenly, the first friend returned and placed the sword at his own neck. "No," said the second friend, "let me die in your place." Deeply moved, the king pardoned both men, asking to be included as a third in their remarkable friendship.

RABBI ADOPH JELLINEK: BET HA-MIDRASH

Enlightenment

"Hear O Israel, the Lord our God, the Lord is One," stated Moses in the Book of Deuteronomy. These six words in Hebrew (known as the *Shema*) are Judaism's most profound gift to mankind's spiritual enlightenment. They unequivocally declare the Oneness of God, the Oneness of the universe, and the Oneness of all humanity. Centuries before the life of Jesus, the Shema was recited daily in the Temple in Jerusalem. To this day, the Shema is recited in Jewish services twice a day. The Gospel of Mark reports that Jesus considered the Shema to be "the most important" commandment.

Inherent in the words of the Shema is the belief that one day all mankind will recognize the Oneness of the One God, bringing about God's kingdom on earth—a world filled with love and justice. Jesus, too, believed that this universal level of spiritual enlightenment would bring about the Kingdom of Heaven on earth.

You are the light of the world. A city on a hill cannot be hidden. Neither do people light a lamp and put it under a bowl. Instead they put it on its stand, and it gives light to everyone in the house. In the same way, let your light shine before men, that they may see your good deeds and praise your Father in heaven.

MATTHEW 5:14-16

I the Lord called you in righteousness,
And I will take hold of your hand,
And I will keep you, and I will make you for a covenant of
    the people,
For a light unto nations—
To open blind eyes,
To free the captive from prison,
And those who sit in darkness from the dungeon.

ISAIAH 42:6-7

What good is it for a man to gain the whole world, yet forfeit his soul?

MARK 8:36

Happy is the man whose hour of death is just like the hour of his birth. Just as he was pure in the hour of his birth, so may he be pure in the hour of his death.

RABBI BEREKHIAH: JERUSALEM TALMUD: MEGILLAH I:9:8L

A time is coming and has come when the true worshippers will worship the Father in spirit and truth.

JOHN 4:23

Whoever is for the Lord, come here.

EXODUS 32:26

I am the light of the world. Whoever follows me will never walk in darkness, but will have the light of life.

JOHN 8:12

Many candles can be kindled from one candle without diminishing its light.

MIDRASH: SIFRE NUMBERS 93

The kingdom of heaven is like to a mustard seed, which a man took and planted in his field. Though it is the smallest of all your seeds, yet when it grows, it is the largest of garden plants and becomes a tree, so that the birds of the air come and perch in its branches.

MATTHEW 13:31-32

So said the Lord God: "I myself will take the top shoot of the cedar and plant it. I will break off a tender twig from its topmost shoots, and I will plant it on a high, lofty mountain. I will plant it in Israel's tall mountains, and it will produce boughs and bear fruit, and it will become a splendid cedar, and birds of all feathers will nest and find shelter in the shade of its branches. And all the trees of the field will know that I the Lord abase the high tree and exalt the low tree. I dry up the green tree, and I make the dry tree flourish."

EZEKIEL 17:22-24

Consider how the lilies of the field grow. They do not labor or spin. Yet I tell you not even Solomon in all his splendor was dressed like one of these.

LUKE 12:27

My beloved went down to his garden,
To the beds of spices,
To feed in the gardens,
And to gather lilies.
I am my beloved's, and my beloved is mine,
Who feeds among the lilies.

THE SONG OF SONGS 6:2-3

Flesh gives birth to flesh, but the Spirit gives birth to spirit.

JOHN 3:6

All heavenly creatures were created from celestial substance; all earthly creatures were created from earthly substance, except man, whose soul is a celestial substance, his body an earthly one. Therefore, if a man keeps the Torah, he is like the creatures above.

RABBI SIMAI: MIDRASH: SIFRE DEUTERONOMY 32:2

Do not store up for yourselves treasures on earth, where moth
and rust destroy, and where thieves break in and steal. But
store up for yourselves treasures in heaven, where moth and
rust do not destroy, and where thieves do not break in and
steal. For where your treasure is, there your heart will be also.

MATTHEW 6:19-21

If you return to the Almighty, you will be restored—
If you hurl unrighteousness from your tent,
And lay your treasure in the dust,
And the gold of Ophir among the stones of the ravines;
The Almighty will be your gold,
And your precious silver;
Then surely you will delight in the Almighty,
And you will lift up your face to God.

JOB 22:23-26

Seek first [God's] kingdom and His righteousness, and all these things will be given to you as well.

MATTHEW 6:33

To follow God, and to find refuge with Him is eternal life.

PHILO, *ON FUGITIVES*, 15:MI

No one can see the kingdom of God unless he is born again.

JOHN 3:3

Man's awakening on earth below awakens a responsive chord in the realm above.

ZOHAR I:86B

Your faith has healed you.

MARK 5:34

I call heaven and earth to witness against you this day: I have put before you life and death, blessing and curse. Choose life—if you and your offspring would live—by loving the Lord your God, heeding His commands, and holding fast to Him.

DEUTERONOMY 30:19-20

I am sending you out like sheep among wolves. Therefore be as shrewd as serpents and as innocent as doves.

MATTHEW 10:16

Brave is the lamb that grazes among seventy wolves.

MIDRASH: YALKUT TO PENTATEUCH 923

Be strong as a leopard, swift as an eagle, fleet as a deer, and strong as a lion in doing the will of your Father in heaven.

JUDAH BEN TEMA: MISHNA: PIRKE AVOT 5:20

The truth will make you free.

JOHN 8:32

Get wisdom, get understanding;
Do not forget and do not veer from the words of my mouth;
Do not forsake her, and she will protect you;
Love her, and she will watch over you.
The beginning of wisdom is: Get wisdom;
But with all your getting, get understanding.
Extol her, and she will exalt you;
She will bring you honor when you embrace her.
She will place a garland on your head,
And give you a crown of glory.

PROVERBS 4:5-9

Again, the kingdom of heaven is like a merchant looking for fine pearls. When he found one of great value, he went away and sold everything he had and bought it.

MATTHEW 13:45-46

It is like a king who has lost a pearl and finds it with the aid of a candle worth only a centime.

MIDRASH: ECCLESIASTES RABBAH 2:11

There is nothing concealed that will not be disclosed, or
hidden that will not be made known.

MATTHEW 10:2

— —

David said to God: "You have created all things in wisdom,
and the greatest thing You have created is the capacity of a
human brain to acquire and retain wisdom. But when I behold
a witless man on the street with torn shirt and bare chest, with
children running after him to torment him, I wonder why You
have permitted a human being to become insane. Why is there
insanity in the universe?"

God answered: "David, I created nothing without purpose.
A time will come when you will see the uses of insanity itself."

When David escaped to Achish (I Samuel 21:14), and
Achish, the King of Gath, wished to slay him, David prayed to
God: "Teach me the madness which You have created." God
instructed him in feigning madness, and David beheld then
that even madness has a purpose.

MIDRASH: SHOKER TOV 34

Everyone who exalts himself will be humbled, and he who humbles himself will be exalted.

LUKE 14:11

My self-abasement is my exaltation, and my self-exaltation is my abasement.

HILLEL: MIDRASH: LEVITICUS RABBAH 1:5

Wisdom

The aphorisms of Jesus and the words of wisdom espoused by the Rabbinic Sages of the Talmud are remarkably alike. Both share an identical message. Jesus said, "The truth will make you free" (John 8:32). The Babylonian Talmud says, "He who has knowledge has everything" (Nedarim 41a). What then is the truth? What must a person understand?

The Talmudic Sage Rabba put it this way: "The goal of wisdom is repentance and good deeds" (Babylonian Talmud: Berakhot 17a). Mankind, created in the spiritual image of God, has the potential to be holy like God, to spread loving-kindness throughout the world. The Babylonian Talmud describes the human soul as the "vital spark of heavenly flame" (Berakhot 10a). Like the Rabbinic Sages, Jesus was determined to impart wisdom on the meek and humble, in the hopes of helping people perfect their own hearts in order to perfect the world.

The Book of Daniel succinctly sums up the shared ethical ideal of both Jesus and Moses: "The wise will shine like the brightness of the heavens, and those who lead the many to righteousness like the stars forever and ever" (Daniel 12:3).

Who of you by worrying can add a single hour to his life?

LUKE 12:25

Be not afraid; for God has come only in order to test you, and in order that the fear of Him may be ever with you, so that you do not go astray.

EXODUS 20:17

If that is how God clothes the grass of the field, which is here today and tomorrow is thrown into the fire, will He not much more clothe you, O you of little faith? So do not worry, saying, "What shall we eat?" or "What shall we drink?" or "What shall we wear?"

MATTHEW 6:30-31

He who has a piece of bread in his basket and asks, "What shall I eat tomorrow?" is among those of little faith.

RABBI ELIEZER MODAI, BABYLONIAN TALMUD: SOTAH 48B

Therefore do not worry about tomorrow, for tomorrow will worry about itself.

MATTHEW 6:34

Do not worry about tomorrow's trouble, for you do not know what a day may bring forth.

BABYLONIAN TALMUD: SANHEDRIN 100B

Do not throw your pearls to pigs.

MATTHEW 7:6

Do not try to sell pearls to those who deal in vegetables and onions.

MIDRASH: TANHUMA: BEHUKOTAI 4

Watch out for false prophets. They come to you in sheep's clothing, but inwardly they are ferocious wolves.

MATTHEW 7:15

The conspiracy of her prophets within her midst is like a roaring lion ravening prey. They devour souls, they take treasure and precious things, they make many widows within her midst. Her priests violate My Teaching and profane what is holy to Me. They do not distinguish between the holy and the ordinary, they do not teach the difference between the unclean and the clean, and they close their eyes to My Sabbaths—so I am profaned among them. Her officials in her midst are like wolves ravening prey—shedding blood and killing souls to win unjust gain.

EZEKIEL 22:25-27

No one pours new wine into old wineskins. If he does, the wine will burst the skins, and both the wine and the wineskins will be ruined. No, he pours new wine into new wineskins.

MARK 2:22

Do not look at the flask, but at what it contains. There may be a new flask full of old wine, and an old flask that does not even contain new wine.

RABBI MEIR: MISHNA: PIRKE AVOT 4:27

The harvest is plentiful but the workers are few.

LUKE 10:2

The day is short, and the work is great, and the workers are sluggish, and the reward is abundant, and the Master of the house is urgent.

RABBI TARFON: MISHNA: PIRKE AVOT 2:20

Blessed are the meek, for they will inherit the earth.

MATTHEW 5:3

The meek will inherit the earth.

PSALM 37:11

If a house is divided against itself, that house cannot stand.

MARK 3:25

A home ruled by dissension will end in destruction.

BABYLONIAN TALMUD: DEREKH ERETZ ZUTA 9

Make a tree good and its fruit will be good, or make a tree bad
and its fruit will be bad, for a tree is recognized by its fruit.
You brood of vipers, how can you who are evil say anything
good? For out of the overflow of the heart the mouth speaks.

MATTHEW 12:33-34

The orchard where the tree grows is judged on the quality of
its fruit, similarly a man's words betray what he feels.

WISDOM OF BEN SIRAH 27:6

Heaven and earth will pass away, but my words will never pass away.

MARK 13:31

Grass withers, the flowers fade,
But the word of our God will stand forever.

ISAIAH 40:8

Suppose one of you wants to build a tower. Will he not first sit down and estimate the cost to see if he has enough to complete it?

LUKE 14:28

Through wisdom a house is built,
And through understanding it is established;
And through knowledge the rooms are filled
With rare and beautiful treasure.

PROVERBS 24:3-4

Stop judging by mere appearances.

JOHN 7:24

The fool sees only the outer garment of a person; the wise man sees his inner garment—his character.

ZOHAR 4:152A

Everyone who hears these words of mine and puts them into practice is like a wise man who built his house on the rock. The rain came down, the streams rose, and the winds blew and beat against that house; yet it did not fall, because it had its foundation on the rock. But everyone who hears these words of mine and does not put them into practice is like a foolish man who built his house on sand. The rain came down, the streams rose, and the winds blew and beat against that house, and it fell with a great crash.

MATTHEW 7:24-27

A man who does good deeds and diligently studies the Torah, to whom is he like? He is like a man who builds a house with a stone foundation and brick walls, so when flood water rise against the walls, that house will not wash away. But a man who does not do any good deeds, even though he studies the Torah, to whom is he like? He is like a man who builds a house with bricks for the foundation and stones above for walls, so even when a little rain falls, the house immediately collapses.

ELISHA BEN ABUYAH: BABYLONIAN TALMUD:
AVOT DE RABBI NATHAN 24:1-2

Foxes have holes and birds of the air have nests, but the Son of
Man has no place to lay his head.

LUKE 9:58

My soul yearns, pines for the courts of the Lord;
My heart and my flesh cry out for the living God.
Even the sparrow has found a house, and the swallow a nest
   for herself,
Where she may lay her young.

PSALM 84:3-4

No prophet is accepted in his hometown.

LUKE 4:24

And Moses spoke up and said: "What if they do not believe me and do not listen to me, but say: The Lord did not appear to you?"

EXODUS 4:1

Study

"Until what period in life should one study Torah?" asks the twelfth century Rabbinic Sage Maimonides in the Mishna Torah. "Until the day of one's death."

In Judaism, studying Torah, believed to be Moses's records of the divine revelation at Mount Sinai, brings people closer to God and inspires them to make the world a better place. For this reason, Jewish tradition glorifies education, holding the scholar in high esteem.

As a teacher, Jesus shared this passion for education, preaching to illiterate Jewish peasants and choosing his disciples from among fishermen. The gospels of the New Testament clearly illuminate Jesus as being exceptionally well versed in Torah, the Psalms, and the writings of the Prophets. Jesus also employed the same teaching method used by rabbis in the synagogues of his time, enhancing his homilies with colorful parables, metaphors, and Biblical references.

"If a man does not pursue Torah," wrote the Rabbinic Sage Simeon ben Lakish, "Torah does not pursue him" (Midrash Mishle 2). With this precept, Jesus would thoroughly agree.

Follow me and I will make you fishers of men.

MARK 1:17

A Rabbi narrates: "I was once accosted by a man who said to me: 'Rabbi, I am entirely unlearned. I do not even know the Torah.'

"I asked him why he did not study, and he replied: 'Because my Father in heaven did not give me understanding and discernment.'

"I said: 'What is your occupation?'

"'I am a fisherman,' he answered.

"'And who taught you to weave nets and to spread them properly for the catch?'

"The fisherman replied: 'Understanding and discernment were given to me from heaven for this purpose.'

"I said: 'If God gave you the understanding to catch fish, did He not give you sufficient intelligence to learn His Torah?'"

MIDRASH: SEDER ELIYAHU 14:196

You are the salt of the earth. But if the salt loses its saltiness, how can it be made salty again? It is no longer good for anything, except to be thrown out and trampled by men.

MATTHEW 5:13

A disciple of the sages should not be like a dish without salt, but should be pleasant to all.

BABYLONIAN TALMUD: KALLAH RABBATI 3:2

No one who puts his hand to the plow and looks back is fit for service in the kingdom of God.

LUKE 9:62

The Lord rained upon Sodom and Gomorrah sulfurous fire from the Lord out of heaven. He annihilated those cities and the entire Plain, and all the inhabitants of the cities and the vegetation of the ground. Lot's wife looked back, and she thereupon turned into a pillar of salt.

GENESIS 19:24-26

Go rather to the lost sheep of Israel.

MATTHEW 10:6

Teach everyone, for many sinners in Israel were led in this way
to study Torah, and from them came righteous, pious, and
worthy men.

BABYLONIAN TALMUD: AVOT DE RABBI NATHAN 2:9

Anyone who does not take his cross and follow me is not worthy of me. Whoever finds his life will lose it, and whoever loses his life for my sake will find it.

MATTHEW 10:38-39

A man does not become worthy to acquire Torah unless he gives his life in its behalf; unless he dispenses with all comforts and pleasures while he strives to attain it. He must be like an ox who permits his master to place a yoke upon him, and who labors for his master without sparing his strength.

MIDRASH: ELIYAHU RABBAH 21

He who has ears, let him hear.

MATTHEW II:I5

If you give your ear to listen a little, you will ultimately hear a lot. If you understand a little, you will ultimately understand a lot.

MIDRASH: SIFRE DEUTERONOMY 79

Woe to you, teachers of the Law and Pharisees, you hypocrites! You shut the kingdom of heaven in men's faces. You yourselves do not enter, nor will you let those enter who are trying to.

Woe to you, teachers of the Law and Pharisees, you hypocrites! You travel over land and sea to win a single convert, and when he becomes one, you make him twice as much a son of hell as you are.

Woe to you, blind guides! You who say, "If anyone swears by the Temple, it means nothing; but if anyone swears by the gold of the Temple, he is bound by his oath". . . .

Woe to you, teachers of the Law and Pharisees, you hypocrites! You give a tenth of your spices—mint, dill, and cumin. But you have neglected the more important matters of the law—justice, mercy, and faithfulness. . . . You blind guides! You strain out a gnat but swallow a camel.

Woe to you, teachers of the Law and Pharisees, you hypocrites! You clean the outside of cup and dish, but inside they are full of greed and self-indulgence. . . .

Woe to you, teachers of the Law and Pharisees, you hypocrites! You are like whitewashed tombs, which look beautiful on the outside, but on the inside are full of dead men's bones and everything unclean. . . .

Woe to you, teachers of the Law and Pharisees, you hypocrites! You build tombs for the Prophets and decorate the graves of the righteous. And you say, "If we had lived in the days of our forefathers, we would not have taken part with them in shedding the blood of the Prophets". . . .

MATTHEW 23:13-30

There are seven types of Pharisees: the "shoulder-Pharisee," who ostentatiously carries the good deeds he has done on his shoulder for all to see; the "wait-a-bit Pharisee," who interrupts his business affairs to say, "Wait a minute, so I can run off and do a good deed"; the "bookkeeping Pharisee," who commits a sin and then does a good deed to balance one against the other; the "miserly Pharisee," who asks, "How can I save some money so I can afford to do a good deed?"; the "show-me-my-sin Pharisee," who says, "Show me what sin I have committed, and I will make up for it by doing an equivalent good deed"; the "Pharisee-out-of-fear," like Job; and the "Pharisee-out-of-love," like Abraham. And the only one dear to God is the Pharisee-out-of-love, like Abraham.

JERUSALEM TALMUD: SOTAH 5:5:2

Come to me, all you who are weary and burdened, and I will give you rest. Take my yoke upon you and learn from me. For I am gentle and humble in heart, and you will find rest for your souls. For my yoke is easy and my burden is light.

MATTHEW 11:28-30

Whoever accepts the yoke of the Torah will be released from the yoke of the kingdom and the yoke of earthly cares.

RABBI NECHUNYA BEN HAKANAH: MISHNA: PIRKE AVOT 3:6

If a blind man leads a blind man, both will fall into a pit.

MATTHEW 15:14

A fool teaches foolishness to his son.

BABYLONIAN TALMUD: SHABBAT 121B

You shall see heaven open, and the angels of God ascending
and descending on the Son of Man.

JOHN 1:51

The voice of the student of the Torah is a ladder on which the
angels ascend and descend.

ZOHAR 4:230B

A student is not above his teacher, nor a servant above his master.

MATTHEW 10:24

Let the honor of your student be as precious to you as your own, and the honor of your colleague be like the reverence for your teacher, and the reverence for your teacher be like the awe of heaven.

RABBI ELAZAR: MISHNA: PIRKE AVOT 4:15

The teachers of the Law and the Pharisees sit in Moses' seat. So you must obey them and do everything they tell you. But do not do what they do, for they do not practice what they preach.

MATTHEW 23:2-3

Some preach well and act well, others act well but do not preach well; you, however, preach well but do not act well.

BABYLONIAN TALMUD: YEBAMOT 63B

A farmer went out to sow his seed. As he was scattering the seed, some fell along the path, and the birds came and ate it up. Some fell on rocky places, where it did not have much soil. It sprang up quickly, because the soil was shallow. But when the sun came up, the plants were scorched, and they withered because they had no root. Other seed fell among thorns, which grew up and choked the plants, so that they did not bear grain. Still other seed fell on good soil. It came up, grew, and produced a crop, multiplying thirty, sixty, or even a hundred times.

MARK 4:3-8

There are four types of disciples: he who quickly understands and quickly forgets, his gain disappears in his loss; he who has difficulty understanding and difficulty forgetting, his loss disappears in his gain; he who understands quickly and has difficulty forgetting, his is a good portion; he who has difficulty understanding and forgets quickly, his is an evil portion.

MISHNA: PIRKE AVOT 5:15

Now the kingdom of heaven is like a landowner who went out early in the morning to hire men to work in his vineyard. He agreed to pay them a denarius for the day and sent them into his vineyard. . . . About the eleventh hour he went out and found still others. He said, "You also go and work in my vineyard."

When evening came, the owner of the vineyard said to his foreman, "Call the workers and pay them their wages . . . ." The workers who were hired about the eleventh hour came and each received a denarius. So when those came who were hired first, they expected to receive more. But each one of them also received a denarius. . . . They began to grumble against the landowner. "These men who were hired last worked only one hour," they said, "and you have made them equal to us who have borne the burden of the work and the heat of the day."

But he answered one of them, "Friend, I am not being unfair to you. Didn't you agree to work for a denarius? . . . I want to give the man who was hired last the same as I gave you."

MATTHEW 20:1-14

A king had a vineyard which he hired workmen to tend. There was one worker there who excelled all the others. When the king saw how efficient he was at his work, he took him by the hand and began to walk up and down with him. At evening the workers came to receive their pay, and that man came with them, and the king gave him the same as all the rest. The workers began to complain, saying, "Your Majesty, we have worked all day, and this man has worked only two or three hours. Is he to receive the same pay as us?" Said the king to them: "Why are you vexed? This man did as much work in two or three hours as you did in the whole day."

MIDRASH: SONG OF SONGS RABBAH 6:6

A man had a fig tree, planted in this vineyard, and he went to look for fruit on it, but did not find any. So he said to the man who took care of the vineyard, "For three years now I've been coming to look for fruit on this fig tree and haven't found any. Cut it down! Why should it use up the soil?"

"Sir," the man replied, "leave it alone for one more year, and I'll dig round it and fertilize it. If it bears fruit next year, fine! If not, then cut it down."

LUKE 13:6-9

A king owned an uncultivated field and said to a worker who lived on his estate, "Go cultivate it and turn it into a vineyard." The worker went and plowed the field and planted a vineyard. The vines grew and yielded wine, but it was sour. When the king discovered the sour wine, he ordered the worker, "Go and cut it all down. What use to me is a vineyard that produces vinegar?" But the worker begged: "O my lord and king, think of all the money you spent before the vineyard was planted, and now you want to cut it all down. Don't say, 'But the wine is sour.' The vineyard is new, and a recently-planted vineyard cannot produce good wine."

MIDRASH: EXODUS RABBAH 43:9

Law

While the laws given by God to Moses at Mount Sinai include the Ten Commandments, a litany of religious ordinances, and the kosher dietary laws, the Torah also instructs Jews to love God, love their neighbors, and pursue justice.

Jesus, who lived during the Talmudic era, actually embraced and advocated interpretations of the laws taught by the Rabbinic Sages of his day. Jesus expected his disciples to observe Jewish law, and his early followers considered themselves Jews and devoted themselves to Torah study. Jesus's disciples prayed at the Temple (Acts 2:46), Peter was strictly kosher (Acts 10:14), and James, the brother of Jesus, insisted that converts to Judaism be "circumcised according to the custom taught by Moses" (Acts 15:1) and commanded Paul of Tarsus to observe the Laws of Moses (Acts 21:24). Paul, however, determined to attract pagan converts to Christianity, insisted that "a man is a Jew if he is one inwardly; and circumcision is circumcision of the heart, by the Spirit, not by the written code" (Romans 2:29) and "a man is justified by faith apart from observing the law" (Romans 3:28). Paul's teaching prevailed, at which point Christianity ceased to be a Jewish sect.

Do not think that I have come to abolish the Law or the Prophets; I have not come to abolish them but to fulfill them. I tell you the truth, until heaven and earth disappear, not the smallest letter, not the least stroke of a pen, will by any means disappear from the Law until everything is accomplished. Anyone who breaks one of the least of these commandments and teaches others to do the same will be called the least in the kingdom of heaven, but whoever practices and teaches these commands will be called great in the kingdom of heaven.

MATTHEW 5:17-19

And now, O Israel, give heed to the laws and rules which I am instructing you to observe, so that you may live to enter and occupy the land that the Lord, the God of your fathers, is giving you. You shall not add anything to what I command you or take anything away from it, but keep the commandments of the Lord your God which I enjoin upon you.

DEUTERONOMY 4:1-2

You have heard that it was said to the people long ago, "Do not murder (Exodus 20:13) and anyone who murders will be subject to judgment." But I tell you that anyone who is angry with his brother will be subject to judgement.

MATTHEW 5:21-22

You shall not hate your kinsman in your heart.

LEVITICUS 19:17

You have heard that it was said, "Do not commit adultery" (Exodus 20:14). But I tell you that anyone who looks at a woman lustfully has already committed adultery with her in his heart.

MATTHEW 5:27-28

You must not suppose that only he who has committed the crime with his body is called an adulterer. He who commits adultery with his eyes is also called an adulterer.

RESH LAKISH: MIDRASH: LEVITICUS RABBAH 23:12

You have heard that it was said to the people long ago, "Do not break your oath, but keep the oaths you have made to the Lord." But I tell you, Do not swear at all; either by heaven, for it is God's throne; or by the earth, for it is His footstool.

MATTHEW 5:33-34

You shall not deal falsely or deceitfully with one another.

LEVITICUS 19:11

No man can serve two masters. Either he will hate the one and love the other, or he will be devoted to the one and despise the other. You cannot serve both God and Money.

LUKE 16:13

You shall not make any gods of silver, nor shall you make for yourselves any gods of gold.

EXODUS 20:20

Haven't you read what David did when he and his companions were hungry (I Samuel 21:1-6)? He entered the house of God, and he and his companions ate the consecrated bread—which was not lawful for them to do, but only for the priests.

MATTHEW 12:3-4

Live by the laws of the Torah, but do not die by them.

BABYLONIAN TALMUD: AVODAH ZARAH 27B

If any one of you has a sheep and it falls into a pit on the Sabbath, will you not take hold of it and lift it out? How much more valuable is a man than a sheep! Therefore it is lawful to do good on the Sabbath.

MATTHEW 12:11-12

Danger to life takes precedence over the sanctity of the Sabbath.

BABYLONIAN TALMUD: SHABBAT 75

If you want to enter life, obey the commandments . . . . Do not murder, do not commit adultery, do not steal, do not give false testimony, honor your father and mother . . . .

MATTHEW 19:17-19

Honor your father and your mother, that you may long endure on the land which the Lord your God is giving you.

You shall not murder.

You shall not commit adultery.

You shall not steal.

You shall not bear false witness against your neighbor.

EXODUS 20:12-13

The Sabbath was made for man, not man for the Sabbath.

MARK 2:27

The Sabbath was given to you, not you to the Sabbath.

SIMON BEN MENASYAH: BABYLONIAN TALMUD: BETZAH 17

So in everything, do to others what you would have them do to you, for this sums up the Law and the Prophets.

MATTHEW 7:12

What is hateful to you, do not do to your neighbor. This is the entire Torah. The rest is commentary. Now go and study it.

HILLEL: BABYLONIAN TALMUD: SHABBAT 31A

Give to Caesar what is Caesar's, and to God what is God's.

MATTHEW 22:21

———

The law of the state is law.

BABYLONIAN TALMUD: BABA KAMA 113A

God

Both Judaism and Christianity worship God as "Father" and believe that people should aspire to be holy by practicing justice and righteousness. Both faiths also believe that humans were created in the spiritual image of God. Judaism, through Moses, originated the notion that there is One God who wants people to rise to His standards of ethical and moral behavior, to have compassion for others, and to observe the Sabbath. Jesus preached these Jewish beliefs, and Christianity, stemming from Judaism, embraced these ideals.

"What does the Lord your God demand of you?" asks Moses in the Torah. "Only this: to revere the Lord your God, to walk only in His paths, to love Him, and to serve the Lord your God with all your heart and soul" (Deuteronomy 10:12-13).

According to Rabbinic literature, "God chose to speak to Moses from a thorn-bush to teach that no place on earth is devoid of the Divine Presence" (Exodus Rabbah 2:5). Similarly, in the New Testament, Jesus compares the kingdom of heaven to a mustard seed. Everything is divinely connected.

And when you pray, do not keep on babbling like the pagans, for they think they will be heard because of their many words. Do not be like them, for your Father knows what you need before you ask him.

MATTHEW 6:7

Do not be reckless with your mouth, and do not let your heart be hasty to utter a word before God; for God is in heaven, and you are on earth, so let your words be few.

ECCLESIASTES 5:1

Our Father in heaven,

hallowed be Your name,

Your kingdom come,

Your will be done on earth as it is in heaven.

MATTHEW 6:9-10

Magnified and hallowed be His great name throughout the world which He has created by His will, and may He bring about His kingdom in your lifetime.

KADDISH: MOURNER'S PRAYER (CIRCA IST CENTURY B.C.E)

Give us today our daily bread.

MATTHEW 6:11

Give me my daily bread.

PROVERBS 30:8

Forgive us our debts, as we also have forgiven our debtors.

MATTHEW 6:12

My children, fill yourselves with compassion, these upon these,
and the Lord will be filled with compassion towards you.

MIDRASH: GENESIS RABBAH 33:3

Lead us not into temptation, but deliver us from evil.

MATTHEW 6:13

Lead us not into sin, iniquity, or temptation.

BABYLONIAN TALMUD: BERAKHOT 60B

Blessed are the pure in heart; for they will see God.

MATTHEW 5:8

Who will ascend the mountain of the Lord?
And who will stand in His holy place?
He who has clean hands and a pure heart.

PSALM 24:3-4

The kingdom of heaven is like yeast that a woman took and mixed in into a large amount of flour until it worked all through the dough.

MATTHEW 13:33

The soul fills the body, just as God fills the universe. The soul sustains the body, just as God sustains the universe. The soul outlasts the body, just as God outlives the universe. The soul is the only one in the body, just as God is the only One in the universe. The soul sees but is not seen, just as God sees but is not seen. The soul is a pure element in the body, just as God is the Pure One in the Universe. The soul in the body never sleeps, just as God never sleeps.

MIDRASH: LEVITICUS RABBAH 4:8

Let the little children come to me, and do not hinder them, for the kingdom of God belongs to such as these. I tell you the truth, anyone who will not receive the kingdom of God like a little child will never enter it.

MARK 10:15

Children receive the radiance of the Divine Presence.

BABYLONIAN TALMUD: KALLAH RABBATI 8

Where two or three come together in my name, there I am with them.

MATTHEW 18:20

If two sit together and they share words of Torah, the Divine Presence is in their midst.

RABBI CHANANYA: MISHNA: PIRKE AVOT 3:3

Why do you call me good? No one is good—except God
alone.

MARK 10:18

Know therefore this day and keep in mind that the Lord alone
is God in heaven above and on earth below; there is no other.

DEUTERONOMY 4:39

With God all things are possible.

MATTHEW 19:26

———

Who is like You, O Lord, among the mighty?
Who is like You, majestic in holiness,
Awesome in splendor, working wonders!

EXODUS 15:11

Do not call anyone on earth "father," for you have one Father, and He is in heaven.

MATTHEW 23:9

There is no father but God.

BABYLONIAN TALMUD: BERAKHOT 35B

For I was hungry and you gave me something to eat, I was thirsty and you gave me something to drink, I was a stranger and you invited me in, I needed clothes and you clothed me, I was sick and you looked after me, I was in prison and you came to visit me.

MATTHEW 25:35-36

And if a man is righteous and does what is just and right: if he does not eat on the mountains, nor lifts up his eyes to the idols of the house of Israel, nor defiles his neighbor's wife, nor lies with a menstruating woman, and if he does not wrong anyone, and returns his pledge for a loan, does not commit robbery, gives bread to the hungry, provides clothing to the naked, he lends without advance interest and does not take accrued interest, refrains from wrongdoing, makes fair judgements between men, follows My laws and keeps My rules, to remain truthful, he is righteous, he will live, declares the Lord God.

EZEKIEL 18:5-9

The kingdom of God does not come with your careful observation, nor will people say, "Here it is" or "There it is," because the kingdom of God is within you.

LUKE 17:20

⸺ ⸺

Let a man always consider himself as if God dwells within him.

BABYLONIAN TALMUD: TAANIT 11B

Justice

"Justice, justice shall you pursue," decrees Moses in the Torah (Deuteronomy 16:20). The word justice is repeated twice not merely to stress the urgency of bringing about justice, but also, according to some interpretations, to emphasize that both the means and the ends must be just. The biblical edict "eye for eye" (Exodus 21:24), frequently misconstrued to advocate retaliation, actually limits vengefulness, insisting that the punishment never be allowed to exceed the crime (not "two eyes for an eye"), but instead that the punishment be appropriate compensation for the eye.

The Hebrew word for justice, *tzedek*, also mean righteousness. "Let justice well up like waters," implores the prophet Amos, "and righteousness like a mighty stream." To be righteous, one must pursue justice and help correct any injustice in the world. One way of achieving this goal is by giving to charity. In fact, the feminine form of the Hebrew word, *tzedaka*, means charity.

While some people contend that Jesus transcended the biblical verse "eye for eye" by exhorting forgiveness, Jesus insists that "With the measure you use, it will be measured to you" (Matthew 7:2)—a standard of justice perfectly in sync with the laws of Moses.

Blessed are they who hunger and thirst for righteousness, for they will be filled.

MATTHEW 5:3

He who pursues righteousness and mercy
Finds life, justice, and honor.

PROVERBS 21:21

When you give to the needy, do not let your left hand know what your right hand is doing, so that your giving may be in secret. Then your Father, who sees what is done in secret, will reward you.

MATTHEW 6:3

He who gives charity in secret is greater than Moses.

RABBI ELEAZAR: BABYLONIAN TALMUD: BAVA BATHRA 9B

Do not judge, and you will not be judged.

LUKE 6:37

He who judges his neighbor on the side of merit is himself judged on the side of merit.

BABYLONIAN TALMUD: SHABBAT 127B

With the measure you use, it will be measured to you.

MARK 4:24

With the measure a man uses, it is measured to him again.

MISHNA: SOTAH I:7

Simply let your "Yes" be "Yes," and your "No," "No."

MATTHEW 5:37

Let your "Yes" be honest, and let your "No" be honest.

RABBI JOSE BEN JUDAH: BABYLONIAN TALMUD:
BAVA METZIA 49A

Enter through the narrow gate. For wide is the gate and broad is the road that leads to destruction, and many enter through it. But small is the gate and narrow the road that leads to life, and only a few find it.

MATTHEW 7:13-14

The path of goodness begins as a thicket of thorns, but soon becomes an open prairie. The path of evil starts as an open prairie, but soon becomes a thicket of thorns.

MIDRASH: SIFRE DEUTERONOMY 11:6

He who is not with me is against me.

LUKE 11:23

If I am not for myself, who will be for me?
And if I am only for myself, what am I?
And if not now, when?

HILLEL: MISHNA: PIRKE AVOT 1:14

The poor you will always have with you, but you will not always have me.

MATTHEW 26:11

For there will never cease to be needy ones in your land, which is why I command you: open your hand to the poor and needy kinsman in your land.

DEUTERONOMY 15:11

A man was going down from Jerusalem to Jericho, when he fell into the hands of robbers. They stripped him of his clothes, beat him and went away, leaving him half dead. A priest happened to be going down the same road, and when he saw the man, he passed by on the other side. So too, a Levite, when he came to the place and saw him, passed by on the other side. But a Samaritan, as he traveled, came where the man was; and when he saw him, he took pity on him. He went to him and bandaged his wounds, pouring on oil and wine. Then he put the man on his own donkey, took him to an inn and took care of him. The next day, he took out two silver coins and gave them to the innkeeper. "Look after him," he said, "and when I return, I will reimburse you for any extra expense you may have."

Which of these three do you think was a neighbor to the man who fell into hands of the robbers?

LUKE 10:30-37

If a man sees his kinsman drowning, mauled by beasts, or attacked by robbers, he is obligated to save him.

BABYLONIAN TALMUD: SANHEDRIN 73A

It is easier for a camel to go through the eye of a needle than for a rich man to enter the kingdom of God.

MARK 10:25

In a dream a man never sees a golden date palm or an elephant going through the eye of a needle.

RABA BAR NACHMANI: BABYLONIAN TALMUD: BERAKHOT 55B

The ground of a certain rich man produced a good crop. He thought to himself, "What shall I do? I have no place to store my crops."

Then he said, "This is what I'll do. I will tear down my barns and build bigger ones, and there I will store all my grain and my goods. And I'll say to myself, "You have plenty of good things laid up for many years. Take life easy; eat, drink, and be merry."

But God said to him, "You fool! This very night your life will be demanded from you. Then who will get what you have prepared for yourself?"

This is how it will be with anyone who stores up things for himself but is not rich toward God.

LUKE 12:16-21

A man kept adding to his store of wine and oil, but never once paid the tithes due from him. What did God do? He caused a spirit of madness to possess the man, causing him to take a stick and begin breaking his jars of wine and oil.

MIDRASH: PESIKTA DE RABBI KAHANA 10:3

If you wish to be perfect, go, sell your possessions and give to the poor, and you will have treasure in heaven. Then come, follow me.

MATTHEW 19:21

Open a hand of compassion to the poor, and God will open to you His store of abundance.

MIDRASH: INTRODUCTION TO TANHUMA, BUBER, 123-4

All who draw the sword will die by the sword.

MATTHEW 26:52

The arrow maker is killed by his own arrows.

BABYLONIAN TALMUD: PESAHIM 28A

Sin

Mankind, endowed with freewill, has the capacity to do both good and evil. The Ten Commandments, revealed by God to Moses at Mount Sinai, double as a checklist of the most serious sins—written in stone.

When Moses descends the mountain with the two tablets, he discovers the Hebrew people worshipping a golden calf. God plans to destroy all those who worshipped the idol, but Moses begs God to either forgive the sins of the people or blot him out. God refuses to allow Moses to suffer for the sins of others. Instead, God sends a plague to punish those who sinned. Those who commit a sin are responsible for their actions and the consequences.

The Talmudic Sages taught that all people sin, that each individual must assume personal responsibility for his or her sins, and that we must constantly struggle to prevent our natural inclination to do evil from triumphing over our natural inclination to do good.

Jesus, too, acknowledged that we all sin, and like the great Talmudic Rabbis, urged people to look inward and take responsibility for their own sins before passing judgment on the sins of others.

Why do you look at the speck of sawdust in your brother's eye and pay no attention to the plank in your own eye?

LUKE 6:41

If the judge said to a man, "Remove the splinter from your eyes," he would reply, "Remove the plank from your eyes."

BABYLONIAN TALMUD: BAVA BATHRA 15B

Follow me, and let the dead bury their own dead.

MATTHEW 8:22

The wicked, even while alive, are considered dead.

BABYLONIAN TALMUD: BERAKHOT 18B

It is not the healthy who need a doctor, but the sick. I have not come to call the righteous, but sinners to repentance.

LUKE 5:31-32

It is the duty of the righteous to aid the wicked, of the wise to aid the unwise, of the rich to aid the poor.

ZOHAR I:208A

If any place will not welcome you or listen to you, shake the dust off your feet when you leave, as a testimony against them.

MARK 6:11

If you warn a wicked man to turn from his way and he does not turn from his way, he will die for his sins, but you will have saved your soul.

EZEKIEL 33:9

My house will be called a house of prayer, but you are making it a den of robbers.

MATTHEW 21:13

Has this house, where My name is called, become a den of robbers in your eyes? Behold, I Myself have seen it, declared the Lord.

JEREMIAH 7:11

What do you think? There was a man who had two sons. He went to the first and said, "Son, go and work today in the vineyard."

"I will not go," he answered, but later he changed his mind and went.

Then the father went to the other son and said the same thing. He answered "I will, sir," but he did not go.

Which of the two did what his father wanted?

MATTHEW 21:28-31

A king had a field which he wished to entrust to métayers. Calling the first, he inquired, "Will you take over this field?" He replied, "I have no strength; the work is too hard for me." In the same way the second, third, and fourth declined to undertake the work. He called the fifth and asked him, "Will you take over this field?" He replied, "Yes." "On the condition that you will till it?" The reply was again, "Yes." But as soon as he took possession of it, he let it fallow. With whom is the king angry?

MIDRASH: EXODUS RABBAH 27:9

There was a landowner who planted a vineyard. He put a wall around it, dug a winepress in it, and built a watchtower. Then he rented the vineyard to some farmers and went away on a journey. When the harvest time approached, he sent his servants to the tenants to collect his fruit.

The tenants seized his servants; they beat one, killed another, and stoned a third. Then he sent other servants to them, more than the first time, and the tenants treated them the same way. Last of all, he sent his son to them. "They will respect my son," he said.

But when the tenants saw the son, they said to each other, "This is the heir. Come, let's kill him and take his inheritance." So they took him and threw him out of the vineyard and killed him.

Therefore, when the owner of the vineyard comes, what will he do to those tenants?

MATTHEW 21:33-40

—

The son of a king committed a terrible crime. His friend told him: "When your father discovers your crime, he will throw you in jail, have you flogged, and feed you only bread and water. Then he will expect you to beg for forgiveness. Listen to me and do the last thing first. Go to him immediately, confess your guilt, and beg for his forgiveness. Hosea gave Israel the same advice: Return to God at once, and protect yourselves from affliction.

MIDRASH: PESIKTA RABBATI 44:4

Watch and pray so that you will not fall into temptation. The spirit is willing, but the body is weak.

MARK 14:38

— —

Man's evil desire gathers strength against him daily and seeks to destroy him. Without God's help, man could not triumph over it.

RABBI SIMEON BEN LEVI: BABYLONIAN TALMUD: KIDDUSHIM 30B

Whoever can be trusted with very little can also be trusted with much, and whoever is dishonest with very little will also be dishonest with much.

LUKE 16:10

Run to do even a slight precept, and flee from sin; for one good deed draws another good deed in its wake, and one sin draws another sin; for the reward of a good deed is another good deed, and the reward of a sin is another sin.

SIMEON BEN AZZAI: MISHNA: PIRKE AVOT 4:2

If any one of you is without sin, let him be the first to throw a stone at her.

JOHN 8:7

He who condemns others condemns himself.

BABYLONIAN TALMUD: KIDDUSHIM 70A

For if men do these things when the tree is green, what will happen when it is dry?

LUKE 23:31

He who is cruel to the compassionate ends by being compassionate to the cruel.

MIDRASH SAMUEL 18

Repentance

In Hebrew, the word for repentance is *teshuvah*, meaning "to return," as in returning to the path of righteousness. In Judaism, if you repent for a sin, are truly remorseful, and change your behavior, then God is forgiving. If, however, you repent for a sin but then continue to commit the sin, then God is unforgiving. Also, God only forgives sins made against God. To repent for a sin made against a fellow human being, you must apologize to that person directly, offering to make amends if necessary. If that person refuses to forgive you, you must offer your apology a total of three times. After that, withholding forgiveness is considered a sin in itself.

Repentance miraculously transforms a sin into a virtue, noted the Talmudic sages, enabling the sincerely repentant person to emerge from harsh self-examination with an amazing feeling of redemption. Jesus beautifully echoes these teachings in his parables and in his attitude toward forgiveness. "Go, and sin no more," Jesus tells a repentant sinner, in harmony with the Jewish concept of *teshuva*. Jesus, like the Talmudic sages, insisted that if a sinner asks for forgiveness with a pure heart, he will be forgiven and will regain his closeness with God. "Return to Me," says God in the Hebrew Bible, "and I will return to you" (Malachi 3:7).

Repent, for the kingdom of heaven is near.

MATTHEW 4:17

Rabbi Eliezer said, "Repent one day before your death."

His disciples asked, "How can a man repent one day before his death if he does not know on which day he will die?"

He replied, "All the more reason to repent today in case he dies tomorrow, and to repent tomorrow in case he dies the next day. So now all his days will be spent in repentance."

BABYLONIAN TALMUD: AVOT DE RABBI NATHAN 15:4

For if you forgive men when they sin against you, your
heavenly Father will also forgive you.

MATTHEW 6:14

Forgive your neighbor's sin against you and then, when you
pray, your sins will be forgiven.

WISDOM OF BEN SIRAH 28:2

If a man owns a hundred sheep, and one of them wanders away, will he not leave the ninety-nine on the hills and go to look for the one that wandered off? And if he finds it, I tell you the truth, he is happier about that one sheep than about the ninety-nine that did not wander off. In the same way your Father in heaven is not willing that any these little ones should be lost.

MATTHEW 18:12-14

There is more joy in heaven over one sinner who repents than over ninety-nine righteous people who need no repentance.

BABYLONIAN TALMUD: SANHEDRIN 99A

I tell you the truth, whatever you bind on earth will be bound in heaven, and whatever you loose on earth will be loosed in heaven.

MATTHEW 18:18

In their youth, Rabbi Simeon ben Lakish and two cohorts were robbers. Rabbi Simeon repented and became a righteous man of great learning. His former partners remained criminals. All three men happened to die on the same day. Rabbi Simeon was sent to paradise, but his former cohorts were sent in the other direction. The two criminals complained, "But the three of us committed robberies together. Why weren't we sent to paradise with Simeon?"

They were told, "Simeon repented and you did not."

"We are ready to repent now," they replied.

The were told, "He who travels through a desert must take along his food, otherwise he will starve. He who goes to sea must carry food, otherwise he will go hungry. The world to come is like both the desert and the sea. No provisions can be obtained there."

MIDRASH: PIRKE DE RABBI ELIEZER 43

There was a man who had two sons. The younger one said to his father, "Father give me my share of the estate." So he divided his property between them.

Not long after that, the younger son got together all he had, set off for a distant country, and there squandered his money in wild living. After he had spent everything, there was a severe famine in that whole country, and he began to be in need. So he went and hired himself out to a citizen of that country, who sent him to his field to feed pigs. He longed to fill his stomach with the pods that the pigs were eating, but no one gave him anything.

When he came to his senses, he said, "How many of my father's hired men have food to spare, and here I am starving to death! I will set out and go back to my father and say to him: Father, I have sinned against heaven and against you. I am no longer worthy to be called your son; make me like one of your hired men." So he got up and went to his father.

But while he was still a long way off, his father saw him and was filled with compassion for him; he ran to his son, threw his arms around him and kissed him.

The son said to him, "Father, I have sinned against heaven and against you. I am no longer worthy to be called your son." But the father said to his servants, "Quick! Bring the best robe and put it on him. Put a ring on his finger and sandals on his feet. Bring the fattened calf and kill it. Let's have a feast and celebrate. For this son of mine was dead and is alive again; he was lost and is found."

LUKE 15:11-24

The son of a king was a hundred days' journey away from his father. His friends said to him, "Return to your father." He replied, "I cannot; I do not have the strength." His father sent word to him, saying, "Come back as far as your strength will allow, and I will go the rest of the way to meet you." So God said to Israel: "Return to Me, and I will return to you" (Malachi 3:7).

MIDRASH: PESIKTA RABBATI 44:9

Two men owed money to a certain moneylender. One owed him five hundred dinarii and the other fifty. Neither of them had the money to pay him back, so he canceled the debts of both. Now which of them will love him more?

LUKE 7:41-42

Two men owe money to a creditor. The first man is a friend, the second man is an enemy. From the friend, the creditor is willing to accept small payments little by little. But from his enemy, he demands payment in one large sum.

RABBI ABBAHU: BABYLONIAN TALMUD: AVODAH ZARAH 4A

Neither do I condemn you. Go now and leave your life of sin.

JOHN 8:11

———

As I live, declared the Lord God, I take no pleasure in the
death of the wicked, but rather when the wicked turn from
their way and live. Turn, turn from your evil ways.

EZEKIEL 33:11

Which of you, if his son asks for bread, will give him a stone?

MATTHEW 7:9

Like a father has compassion on his children,
So the Lord has compassion on those who fear Him.

PSALM 103:13

Differences

The New Testament does not reveal how Jesus acquired his extensive knowledge of Judaism. Some scholars suggest that Jesus may have actually been a disciple of the great rabbinic sage Hillel, revered as one of the great teachers of his time, who died around 20 C.E.

While many of the ethical teachings, ideas, and values expressed by Jesus bear a remarkable resemblance to the those of Hillel, a handful of radical teachings attributed to Jesus contradict Jewish teachings.

Jesus preached to turn the other cheek—a beautiful call for nonviolence embraced by Judaism to a degree, but not to the point of sacrificing one's life or allowing evil to flourish. Jesus insisted that people need him as an intermediary to get close to God; Judaism insists that no one needs an intermediary to confront God directly. Jesus claimed that the kosher dietary laws are superfluous; Judaism insists that the Torah has never been superseded. Jesus exalted poverty as a means to greater spirituality; Mosaic tradition forbids a person from pauperizing himself. Jesus forbids remarriage after divorce except in cases of adultery; Jewish law allows divorce for any reason.

You have heard that it was said, "Eye for eye, and tooth for tooth" (Exodus 21:24). But I tell you, do not resist an evil person.

MATTHEW 5:38-39

You will sweep out evil from your midst.

DEUTERONOMY 13:6

All things have been committed to me by my Father. No one knows who the Son is except the Father, and no one knows who the Father is except the Son and those to whom the Son chooses to reveal Him.

LUKE 10:22

All who have real knowledge of the one Creator and Father of all things are rightly called sons of God.

PHILO, *ON THE CONFUSION OF LANGUAGES* 28:M1

What goes into a man's mouth does not make him unclean,
but what comes out of his mouth, that is what makes him
unclean.

MATTHEW 15:11

You shall not eat anything abhorrent.

DEUTERONOMY 14:3

For the Son of Man is going to come in his Father's glory with
his angels, and then he will reward each person according to
what he has done.

MATTHEW 16:27

I the Lord search the heart,
Test the minds,
And reward every man according to his conduct,
According to the fruit of his deeds.

JEREMIAH 17:10

What God has joined together, let man not separate. . . .
Moses permitted you to divorce your wives because your
hearts were hard. But it was not this way from the beginning.
I tell you that anyone who divorces his wife, except for marital
unfaithfulness, and marries another woman commits adultery.

MATTHEW 19:6, 8-9

The School of Shammai says a man should not divorce his
wife unless he has found her guilty of some unseemly act, as
the Torah says, "because he has found something unseemly in
her" (Deuteronomy 24:1).

The School of Hillel, however, says a man may divorce his
wife even if she has merely spoiled his food, since the Torah
says, "because he has found something unseemly in her."

Rabbi Akiva says a man may divorce his wife even if he
finds another woman more beautiful than she is, as the Torah
says, "if it comes to pass, she finds no favor in his eyes."

MISHNA: GITTIN 90A

I tell you the truth, this poor widow has put more into the treasury than all the others. They all gave out of their wealth; but she, out of her poverty, put in everything—all she had to live on.

MARK 12:43-44

Giving charity is an obligation, but it has limits. For a man to give away all his possessions and make himself a pauper is forbidden.

BABYLONIAN TALMUD: KETHUBOT 50A

Be perfect, therefore, as your heavenly Father is perfect.

MATTHEW 5:48

You shall be holy, for I, the Lord your God, am holy.

LEVITICUS 19:2

Hereafter

Both Judaism and Christianity believe that each individual has an immortal soul. During the time of the rabbis of the Talmud, which overlapped the lifetime of Jesus, Jewish doctrine held that when a person dies, the soul is reunited with God—until the Messianic age, at which time the bodies of the dead are resurrected and their souls return to them. Jesus clearly embraced this doctrine of resurrection, a doctrine still accepted today by Orthodox Judaism but rejected by Conservative and Reform Judaism.

To Jewish thinkers, the eternity of the hereafter cannot be understood in terms of the time and space of the material world we currently inhabit. The soul does not merely go to heaven, it becomes a part of heaven—a dimension outside the confines of time and beyond the scope of human comprehension.

The kingdom of heaven, as described by Jesus, is the same kingdom of heaven described by the Prophets of the Hebrew Bible and by the rabbis of the Talmud. It is a kingdom of heaven on earth, a time of universal peace, brotherhood, and love.

Blessed are the poor in spirit, for theirs is the kingdom of heaven.

MATTHEW 5:3

He who suffers on earth will be free in the world to come.

MIDRASH: GENESIS RABBAH 92:1

Unless your righteousness surpasses that of the Pharisees and the teachers of the Law, you will certainly not enter the kingdom of heaven.

MATTHEW 5:20

When a man stands before the throne of judgment, the first question he is asked is: "Were you honest in all your dealings with other people?"

RABA BAR NACHMANI: BABYLONIAN TALMUD: SHABBAT 31A

The kingdom of heaven is like a treasure hidden in a field. When a man found it, he hid it again, and then in his joy went and sold all he had and bought that field.

MATTHEW 13:44

Rabbi Johanan was walking from Tiberias to Sepphoris with Rabbi Hiyya bar Abba. When they passed a farm, Rabbi Johanan said, "I once owned this farm, but I sold it to devote my life to studying Torah." When they passed a vineyard, Rabbi Johanan said, "I once owned this vineyard, but I sold it to devote my life to studying Torah." When they passed an olive orchard, Rabbi Johanan said, "I once owned this olive orchard, but I sold it to devote my life to studying Torah."

Suddenly Rabbi Hiyya began to cry.

"Why are you crying?" asked Rabbi Johanan.

Rabbi Hiyya answered, "I weep because you did not put anything aside for your old age."

"Hiyya, my son, is what I did really that foolish?" asked Rabbi Johanan. "I gave up something that was made in six days to acquire something that was made in forty days and forty nights. For God created the entire world in six days, but to give the Torah He took forty days and forty nights."

MIDRASH: PESIKTA DE RABBI KAHANA 27:1

The kingdom of heaven is like a man who sowed good seed in his field. But while everyone was sleeping, his enemy came and sowed weeds among the wheat, and went away. When the wheat sprouted and formed heads, then the weeds also appeared.

The owner's servants came to him and said, "Sir, didn't you sow good seed in your field? Where then did the weeds come from?"

"An enemy has done this," he replied.

The servants asked, "Do you want us to pull them out?"

"No," he answered, "because while you are pulling the weeds, you may root up the wheat with them. Let both grow together until the harvest. At that time I will tell the harvesters: First collect the weeds and tie them in bundles to be burned; then gather the wheat and bring it into my barn."

MATTHEW 13:24-30

A king, while visiting his garden, gave orders that the thorns be torn out, but, when he observed budding roses among them, he left the thorns because of the roses. When the flowers grew and were plucked, he ordered that the thorns be removed.

MIDRASH: ZOHAR HADASH I:12B

Not everyone who says to me, "Lord, Lord," will enter the kingdom of heaven, but only he who does the will of my Father who is in heaven.

MATTHEW 7:21

What does the Lord require of you, but to do justly, and to love mercy, and to walk humbly with your God?

MICAH 6:8

A certain man was preparing a great banquet and invited many guests. At the time of the banquet he sent his servant to tell those who had been invited, "Come, for everything is now ready."

But they all alike began to make excuses. The first said, "I have just bought a field, and I must go and see it. Please excuse me." Another said, "I have just bought five yoke of oxen, and I'm on my way to try them out. Please excuse me." Still another said, "I just got married, so I can't come."

The servant came back and reported this to his master. Then the owner of the house became angry and ordered his servant, "Go out quickly into the streets and alleys of the town and bring in the poor, the crippled, the blind, and the lame."

"Sir," the servant said, "what you ordered has been done, but there is still room."

Then the master told his servant, "Go out to the roads and country lanes and make them come in, so that my house will be full. I tell you, not one of those men who were invited will get a taste of my banquet."

LUKE 14:16-24

A king invited his subjects to a banquet without specifying the time. The wise ones dressed up and sat at the door of the palace, saying, "a royal palace has everything, so the door may open at any moment." The fools continued working, saying, "how can there be a banquet without preparations?" Suddenly the king summoned his subjects. The wise entered adorned in their fine clothes, but the fools entered wearing soiled clothes. The king delighted over the wise, but he was angry with the fools. "Those who dressed for the banquet," he announced, "may sit, eat, and drink. But those who did not dress for the banquet, must stand and watch."

RABBI JOHANAN BEN ZAKKAI: BABYLONIAN TALMUD:
SHABBAT 153A

The kingdom of heaven is like a net that was let down into the lake and caught all kinds of fish. When it was full, the fisherman pulled it up on shore. Then they sat down and collected the good fish in baskets, but threw the bad away.

MATTHEW 13:47-48

Everything is given on pledge, and a net is spread over all the living; the shop is open, and the dealer gives credit; the ledger lies open, and the hand writes; and whoever wishes to borrow may come and borrow; but the collectors regularly make their daily round and exact payment from man, with or without his consent; and they have that whereon they can rely in their demand; and the judgement is a judgment of truth; and everything is prepared for the feast.

RABBI AKIVA: MISHNA: PIRKE AVOT 3:20

When the dead rise, they will neither marry nor be given in marriage; they will be like the angels in heaven.

MARK 12:25

In the world to come, there is no eating, drinking, marrying, envy, jealousy, hatred, or strife. Instead, the righteous sit with crowns on their heads, basking in the brilliance of the Divine Presence.

RABH: BABYLONIAN TALMUD: BERAKHOT 17A

Now about the dead rising—have you not read in the book of
Moses, in the account of the bush (Exodus 3:6), how God
said to him: "I am the God of Abraham, the God of Isaac,
and the God of Jacob"? He is not the God of the dead, but of
the living.

MARK 12:26-27

How do we know that the dead speak with each other? Because
Scripture tells us that immediately before Moses died, the
Lord said to Moses, "This is the land I swore to Abraham,
Isaac, and Jacob, saying 'I will give it to your offspring'"
(Deuteronomy 34:4). Why does God use the word "saying"?
Because God was actually instructing Moses to "Tell
Abraham, Isaac, and Jacob that the oath I swore to them I have
already carried out for their descendants." Now if you insist
that the dead have no awareness, why would Moses need to tell
them anything?

BABYLONIAN TALMUD: BERAKHOT 18B-19A

And the nations will be gathered before him, and he will separate the people one from another as a shepherd separates the sheep from the goats.

MATTHEW 25:32

As for you, My flock, the Lord God says this: Look, I judge between sheep and sheep, between the rams and between the goats.

EZEKIEL 34:17

I have other sheep that are not of this sheep pen.

JOHN 10:16

— —

Are you not just like the Ethiopians to Me, children of Israel?—declares the Lord. Did I not bring up Israel from the land of Egypt, and the Philistines from Caphtor, and the Syrians from Kir?

AMOS 9:7

In my Father's house are many rooms.

JOHN 14:2

This world is like an antechamber to the world to come; prepare yourself in the antechamber so you may enter the banquet hall.

RABBI JACOB: MISHNA: PIRKE AVOT 4:21

Bibliography

Quotes

CHRISTIAN QUOTES
Holy Bible, New International Version, by International Bible Society (Zondervan Publishing House, 1984).

JEWISH QUOTES
The Torah
    The Torah: The Five Books of Moses (Philadelphia: Jewish Publication Society of America, 1962).

The Prophets and the Writings
    JPS Hebrew-English Tanakh: The Traditional Hebrew Text and The New JPS Translation (Philadelphia: Jewish Publication Society of America, 1999).

The Wisdom of Ben Sirah
    The Jerusalem Bible (Garden City, New York: Doubleday, 1966).

Philo
    The Works of Philo, translated by C.D. Yonge (Peabody, Massachusetts: Hendrickson, 1993).

The Testaments of the Twelve Patriarchs
    The Old Testament Pseudepigrapha, Volumes 1 & 2, edited by James H. Charlesworth (New York: Doubleday, 1983).

Babylonian Talmud

    Hebrew-English Edition of the Babylonian Talmud, translated by Rabbi B. D. Klein, B.A. (London: The Soncino Press, 1985).

Jerusalem Talmud

    The Talmud of the Land of Israel, translated by Jacob Neusner (Chicago: The University of Chicago Press, 1985).

Midrash

    Bet ha-Midrash, by Rabbi Adoph Jellinek (Leipsic and Vienna, 1853-1877).

    Midrash Mishle, by S. Buber (Vilna, 1893).

    Midrash Rabbah (London: The Soncino Press, 1983).

    Midrash Tanhuma, translated by John T. Townsend (Hoboken, New Jersey: Ktav Publishing House, 1997).

    Pesikta de-Rab Kahana, translated by William G. Braude and Israel J. Kapstein (Philadelphia: Jewish Publication Society of America, 1975).

    Pesikta Rabbati, translated from the Hebrew by Rabbi William G. Braude (New Haven: Yale University Press, 1968).

    Tanna Debe Eliyyahu: The Love of the School Elijah, translated from the Hebrew by William G. Braude and Israel J. Kapstein (Philadelphia: Jewish Publication Society of America, 1981).

Zohar

    The Zohar, translated by Harry Speling and Maurice Simon (London: The Soncino Press, 1984).

Reference

Biblical Literacy, by Rabbi Joseph Telushkin (New York: William Morrow, 1997).

The Book of Jewish Knowledge, by Nathan Ausubel (New York: Crown, 1964).

Christianity in Talmud and Midrash, by R.T. Herford (London, 1903).

Exploring Exodus, by Nahum M. Sarna (New York: Schocken Books, 1986).

The Gospel According to Jesus, by Stephen Mitchell (New York: HarperCollins, 1991).

Gospel Parables in Light of Jewish Background, by W.O.E. Oesterley (New York, 1936).

Jesus and the Law in Synoptic Tradition, by Robert Banks (Cambridge: Cambridge University Press, 1975).

Jesus in Talmud, Midrash, Zohar and Synagogue, by G. Dalman (Cambridge, 1893).

Jesus of Nazareth, by Joseph Klausner (New York: Macmillan, 1925).

Jewish Literacy, by Rabbi Joseph Telushkin (New York: William Morrow, 1991).

The Jewish Sources of the Sermon on the Mount, by Gerald Friedlander (London: Ktav, 1911).

The Sabbath in Jewish and Christian Tradition, edited by Tamara Eskenazi, Daniel Harrington, and William Shea (New York: Crossroad, 1991).

The Talmudic Anthology: Tales & Teachings of the Rabbis, edited by Louis I. Newman with Samuel Spitz (West Orange, New Jersey: Behrman House, 1945). Pages 60, 65, 75, 85, 262-263, 273, 308, 341, 358, 380, 453, 502, 506.

A Rabbi Talks with Jesus, by Jacob Neusner (New York: Doubleday, 1993).

They Also Taught in Parables, by Harvey K. McArthur and Robert M. Johnston (Grand Rapids, Michigan: Academie Books, 1990).

Index of Quotes

New Testament

Torah

Prophets & Writings

Wisdom of Ben Sirah

Philo

Testaments of the Twelve Patriarchs

Mishna

Babylonian Talmud

JOEY GREEN, the author of more than twenty books, including *The Zen of Oz* and *The Road to Success Is Paved with Failure*, has appeared on "The Tonight Show with Jay Leno," "The Rosie O'Donnell Show," "Today," "The View," "The Conan O'Brien Show," "Dateline NBC," and "Good Morning, America." He has been profiled in the *New York Times, People, Entertainment Weekly*, and *The Los Angeles Times*. A former contributing editor to *National Lampoon* and a former advertising copywriter at J. Walter Thompson, Green is a graduate of Cornell University, practices Judaism, and backpacked around the world for two years on his honeymoon. He lives in Los Angeles with his wife, Debbie, and their two daughters, Ashley and Julia.

RABBI STEWART VOGEL, who penned the introduction, is the spiritual leader of Temple Aliyah in Woodland Hills, California. He is the co-author of the national bestseller *The Ten Commandments: The Significance of God's Laws in Everyday Life*. For twenty years he has been involved in interfaith work and was honored by the National Conference of Christians and Jews. Rabbi Vogel is the past president of the Rabbinical Assembly—Western Region and is widely recognized as a dynamic speaker, teacher, and synagogue leader. He lives in Los Angeles with his wife, Rodi, and their four children, Talya, Elie, Ari, and Avi.